1 PIANO, 4 HANDS

CHART HITS FOR EASY DUET

Arranged by
ERIC BAUMGARTNER

INCLUDES ONLINE AUDIO

The online audio tracks give you the flexibility to rehearse or perform these piano duets anytime and anywhere. Each piece features a Secondo part, a Primo part, and a demo track of both parts together that can be downloaded or streamed. The *PLAYBACK+* feature allows you to change the tempo without altering the pitch.

PLAYBACK+
Speed · Pitch · Balance · Loop

To access audio visit:
www.halleonard.com/mylibrary

Enter Code
6674-7132-0383-4730

ISBN 978-1-4950-6319-0

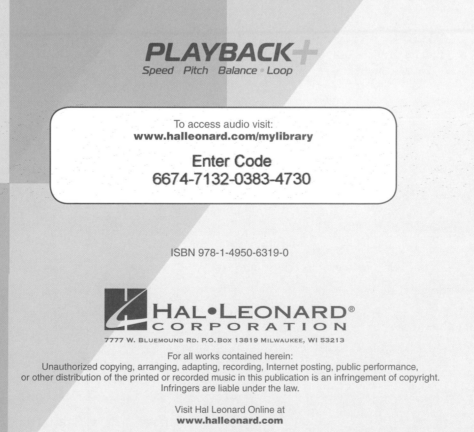

HAL•LEONARD®
CORPORATION

7777 W. BLUEMOUND RD. P.O. BOX 13819 MILWAUKEE, WI 53213

Visit Hal Leonard Online at
www.halleonard.com

ALL OF ME

SECONDO

Words and Music by JOHN STEPHENS
and TOBY GAD

Moderately, with feeling

p sempre legato

(melody)
mp

With pedal

ALL OF ME

PRIMO

Words and Music by JOHN STEPHENS
and TOBY GAD

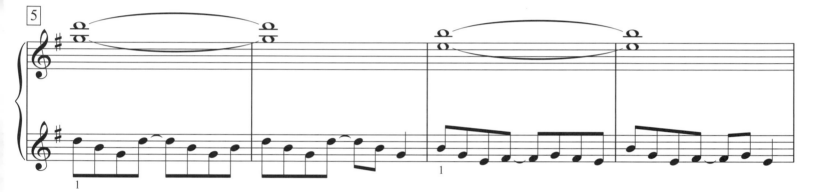

SECONDO

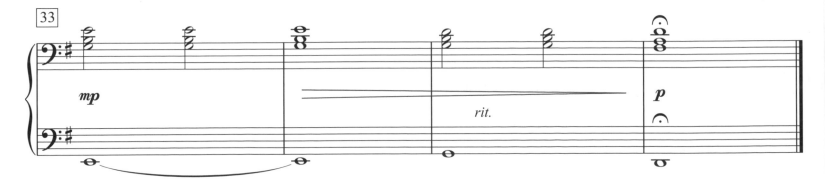

PRIMO

GRENADE

SECONDO

Words and Music by BRUNO MARS,
ARI LEVINE, PHILIP LAWRENCE,
BRODY BROWN, CLAUDE KELLY
and ANDREW WYATT

GRENADE

PRIMO

Words and Music by BRUNO MARS,
ARI LEVINE, PHILIP LAWRENCE,
BRODY BROWN, CLAUDE KELLY
and ANDREW WYATT

Moderately fast

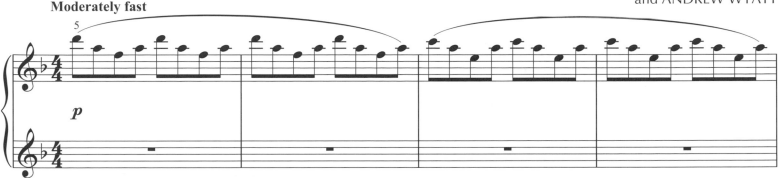

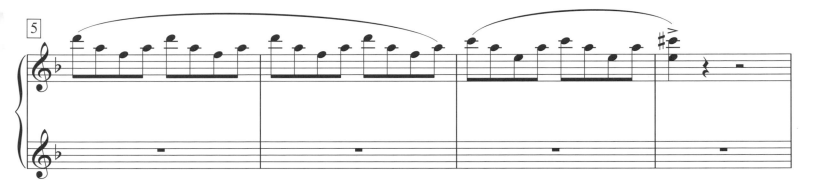

SECONDO

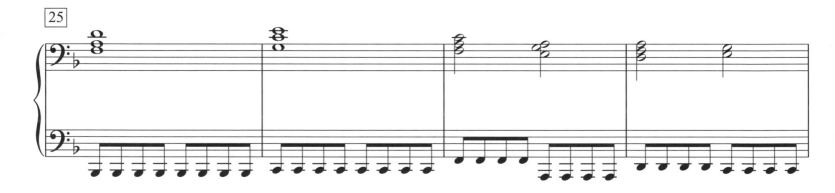

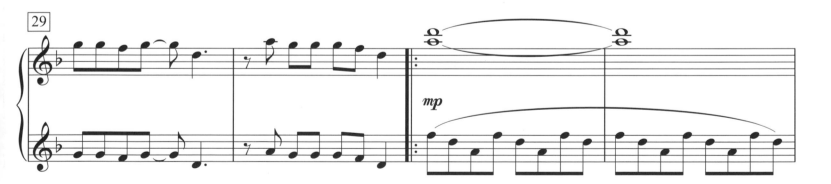

HAPPY
from DESPICABLE ME 2

SECONDO

Words and Music by
PHARRELL WILLIAMS

Moderately fast

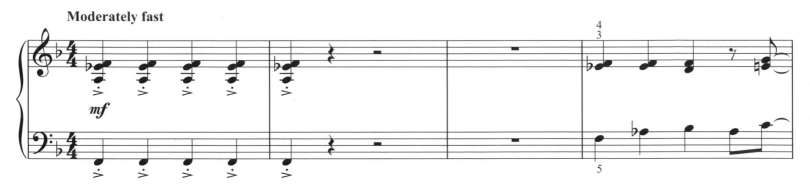

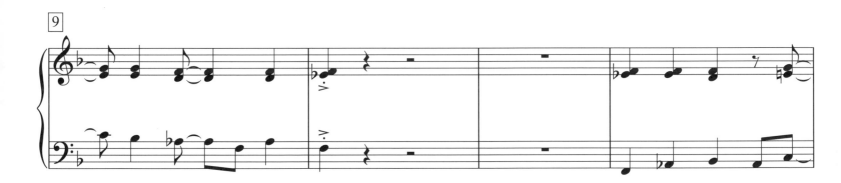

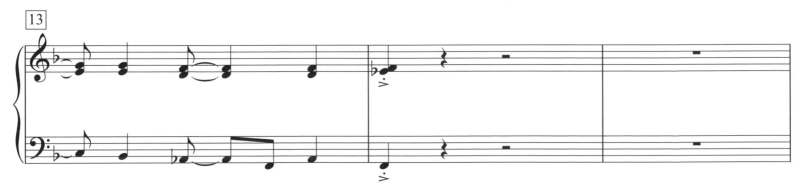

HAPPY
from DESPICABLE ME 2

PRIMO

Words and Music by
PHARRELL WILLIAMS

Moderately fast

PRIMO

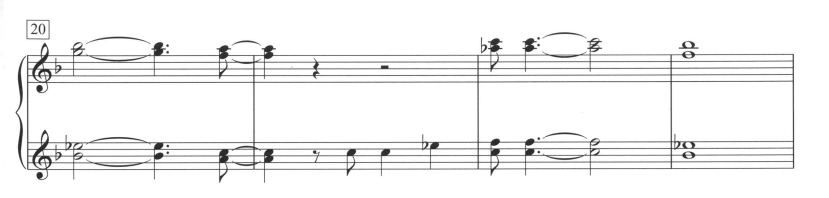

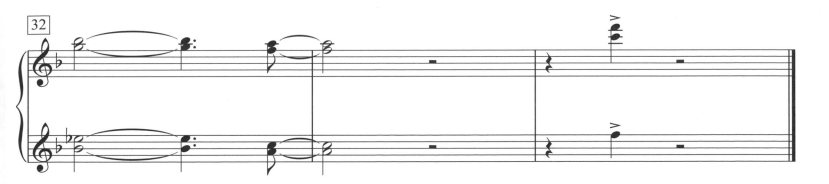

HELLO

SECONDO

Words and Music by ADELE ADKINS
and GREG KURSTIN

Moderately slow

HELLO

PRIMO

Words and Music by ADELE ADKINS
and GREG KURSTIN

Moderately slow

R.H. second time only

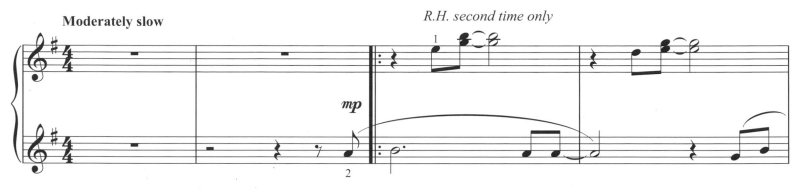

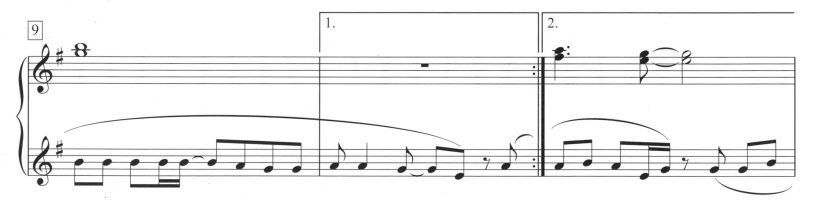

SECONDO

PRIMO

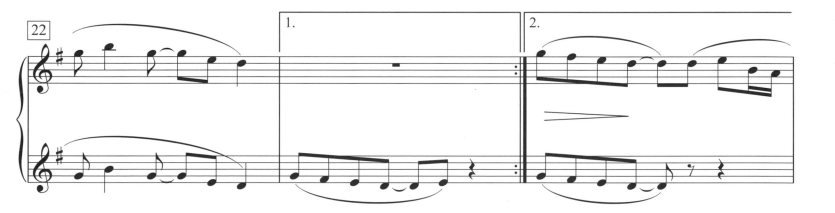

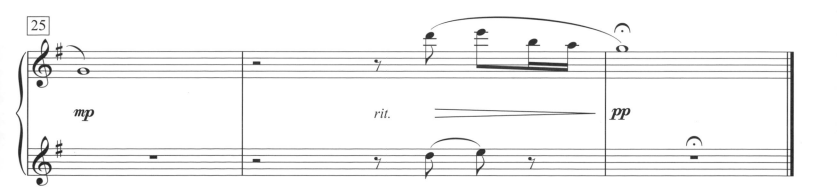

JUST GIVE ME A REASON

SECONDO

Words and Music by ALECIA MOORE,
JEFF BHASKER and NATE RUESS

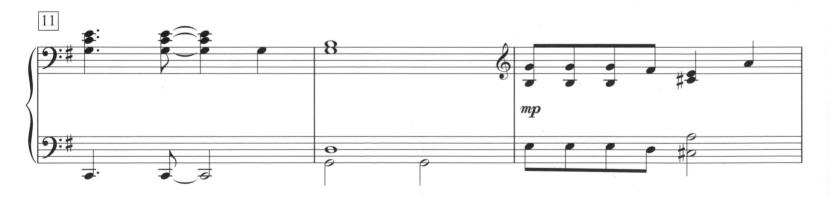

JUST GIVE ME A REASON

PRIMO

Words and Music by ALECIA MOORE,
JEFF BHASKER and NATE RUESS

Moderately

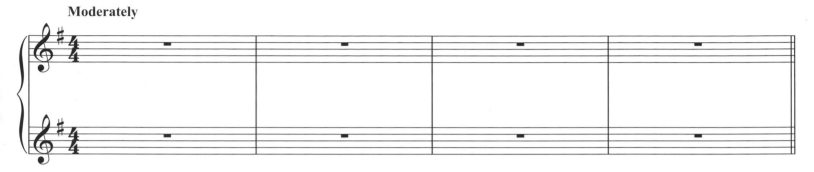

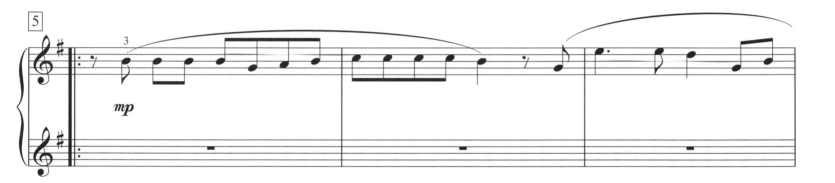

SECONDO

PRIMO

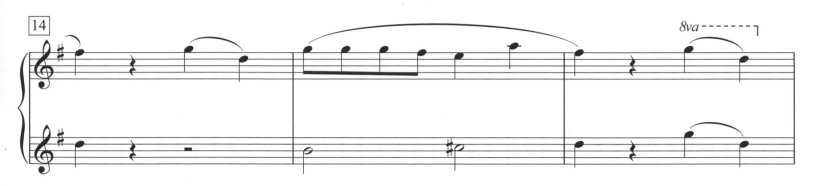

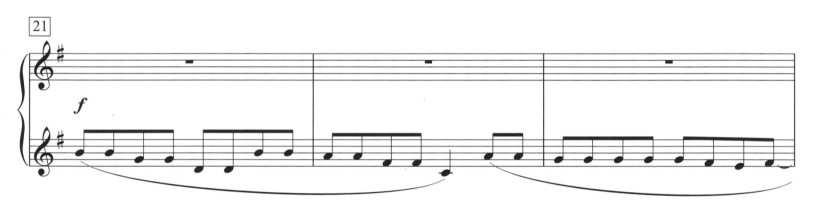

SECONDO

PRIMO

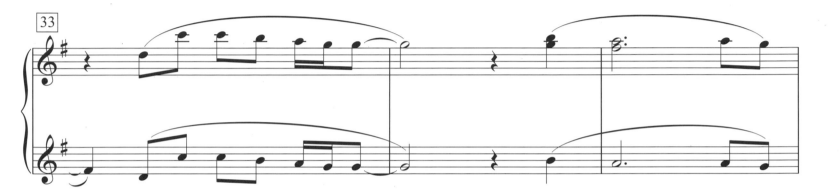

ROAR

SECONDO

Words and Music by KATY PERRY,
LUKASZ GOTTWALD, MAX MARTIN,
BONNIE McKEE and HENRY WALTER

Moderate Pop

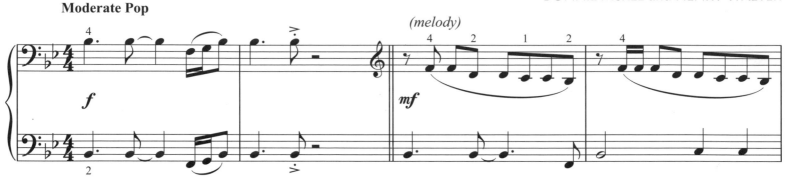

ROAR

PRIMO

Words and Music by KATY PERRY,
LUKASZ GOTTWALD, MAX MARTIN,
BONNIE McKEE and HENRY WALTER

Moderate Pop

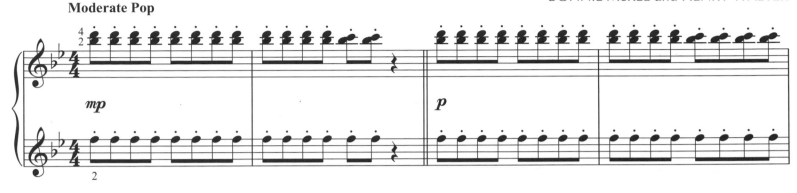

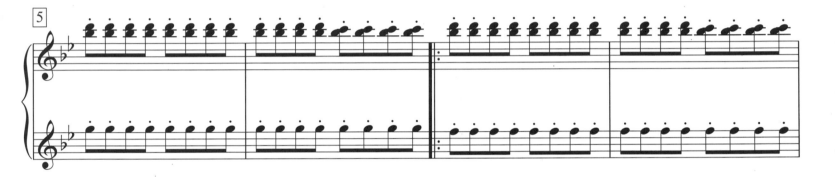

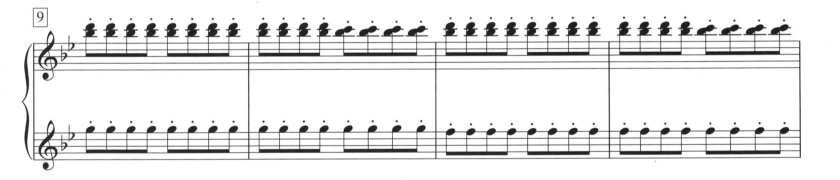

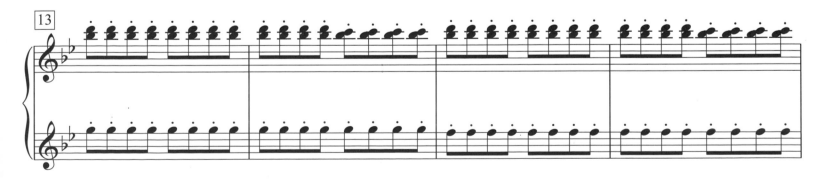

SECONDO

PRIMO

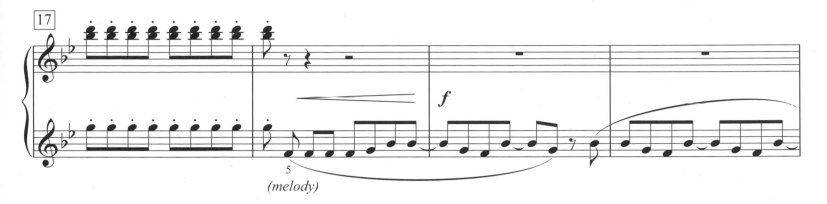

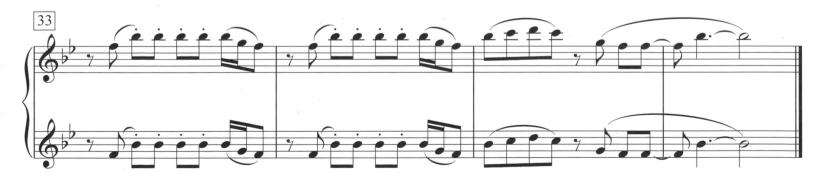

SHAKE IT OFF

SECONDO

Words and Music by TAYLOR SWIFT,
MAX MARTIN and SHELLBACK

Fast beat

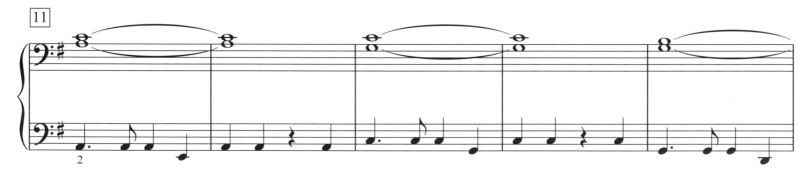

SHAKE IT OFF

PRIMO

Words and Music by TAYLOR SWIFT,
MAX MARTIN and SHELLBACK

SECONDO

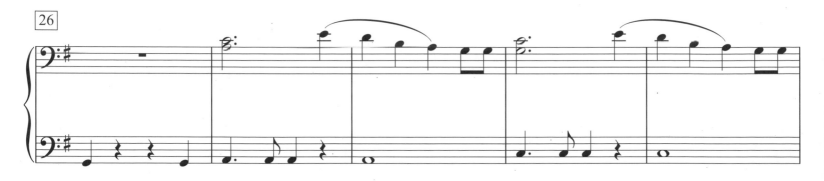

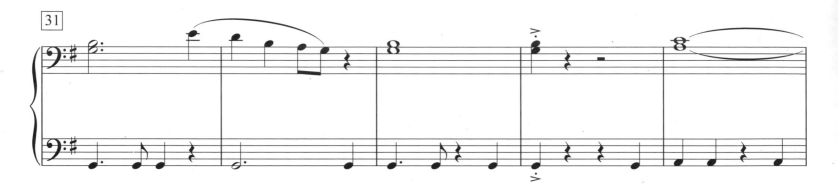

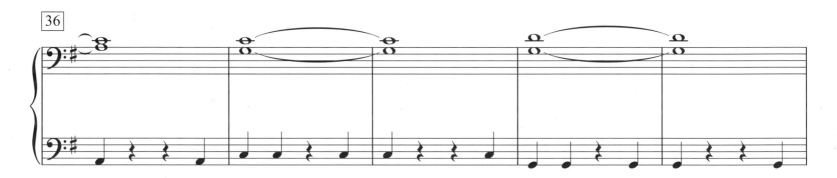

PRIMO

STAY

SECONDO

Words and Music by MIKKY EKKO
and JUSTIN PARKER

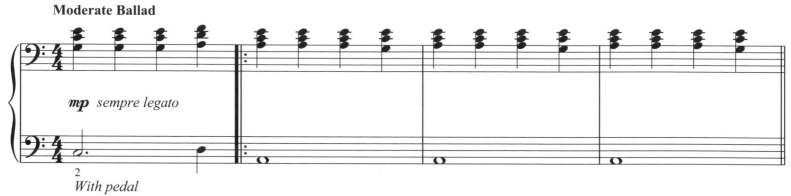

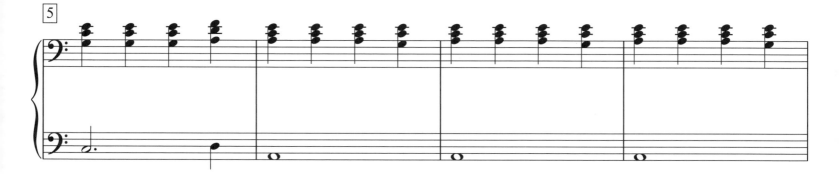

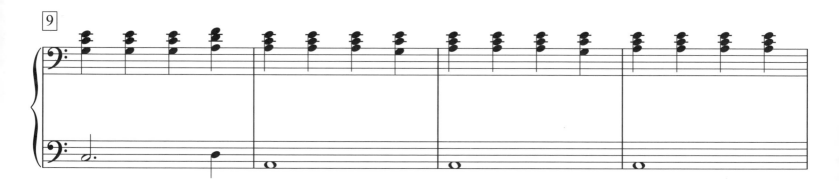

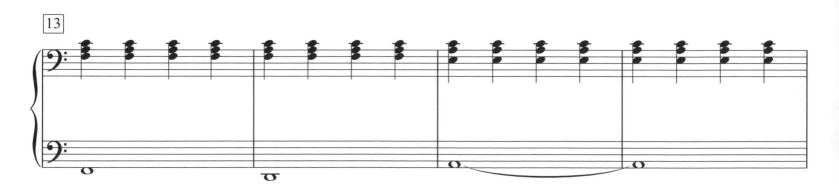

STAY

PRIMO

Words and Music by MIKKY EKKO
and JUSTIN PARKER

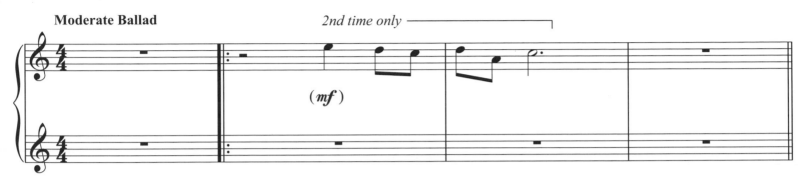

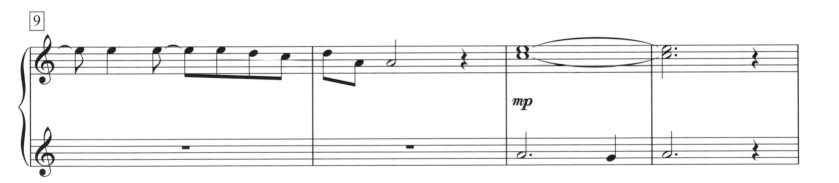

SECONDO

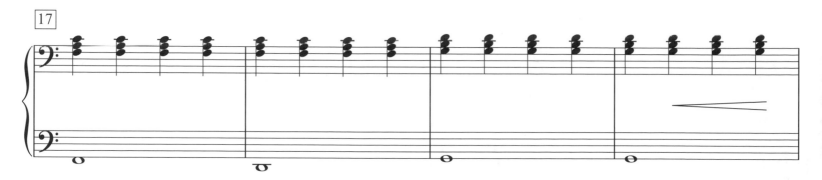

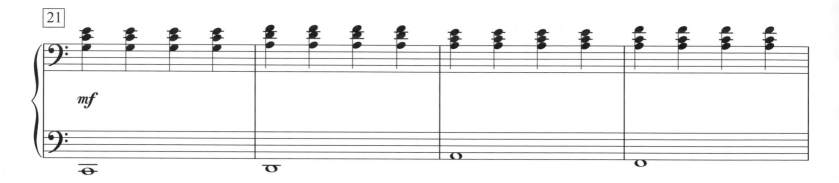

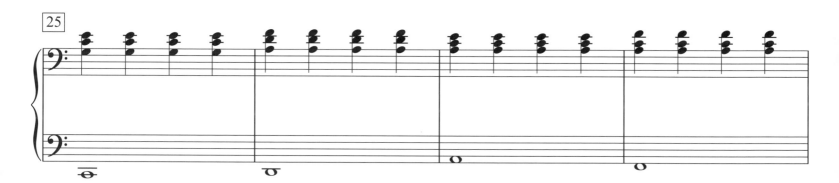

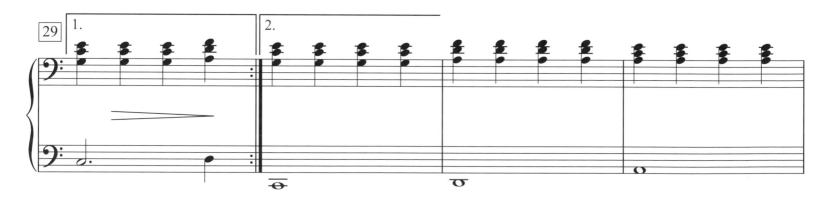

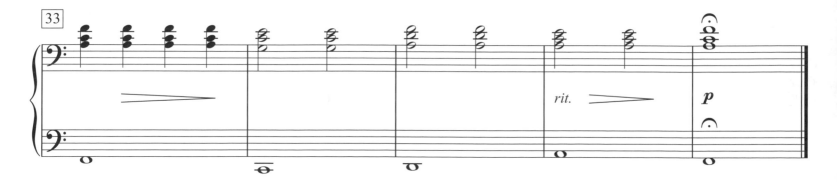

PRIMO

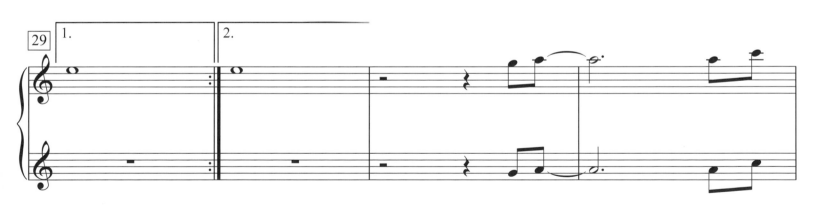

STAY WITH ME

SECONDO

Words and Music by SAM SMITH,
JAMES NAPIER, WILLIAM EDWARD PHILLIPS,
TOM PETTY and JEFF LYNNE

Moderate Soul

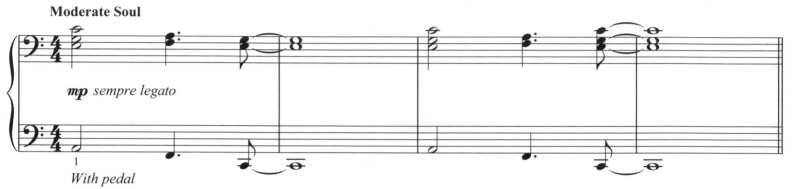

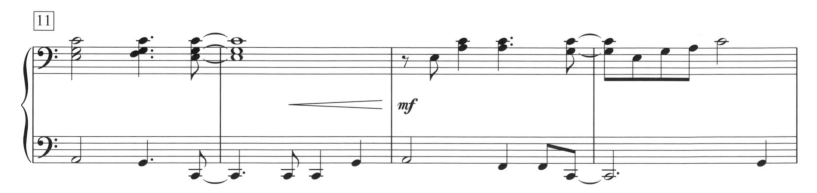

STAY WITH ME

PRIMO

Words and Music by SAM SMITH,
JAMES NAPIER, WILLIAM EDWARD PHILLIPS,
TOM PETTY and JEFF LYNNE

Moderate Soul

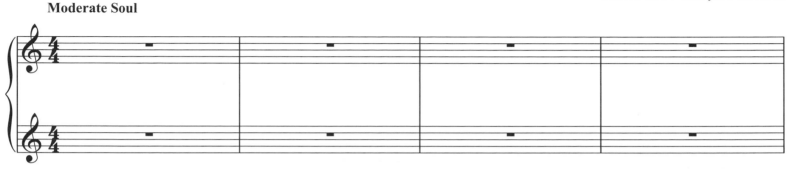

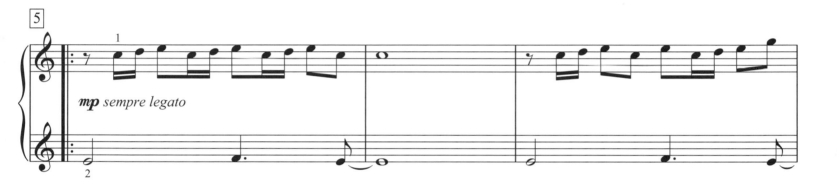

SECONDO

PRIMO

THINKING OUT LOUD

SECONDO

Words and Music by ED SHEERAN
and AMY WADGE

Moderately

THINKING OUT LOUD

PRIMO

Words and Music by ED SHEERAN
and AMY WADGE

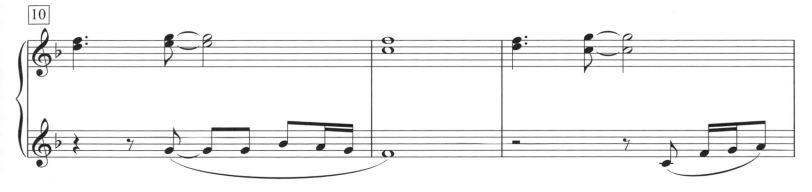

SECONDO

PRIMO

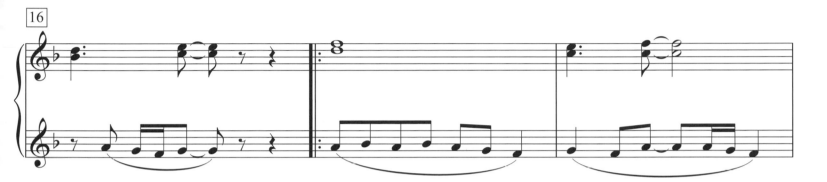

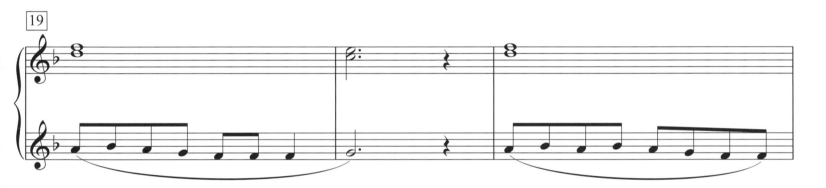

SECONDO

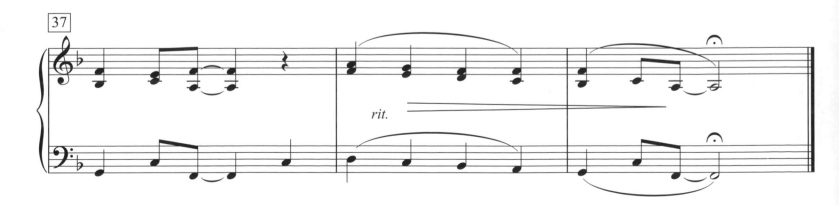

PRIMO

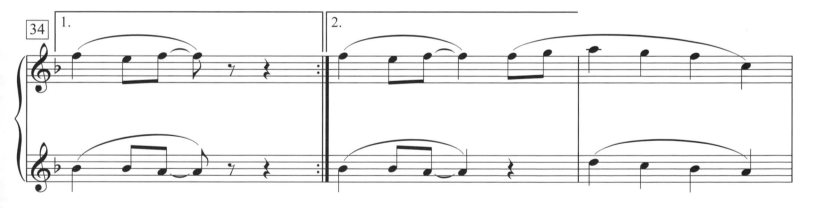

PIANO FOR TWO
A Variety of Piano Duets from Hal Leonard

ADELE FOR PIANO DUET
Intermediate Level

Eight of Adele's biggest hits arranged especially for intermediate piano duet! Featuring: Chasing Pavements • Hello • Make You Feel My Love • Rolling in the Deep • Set Fire to the Rain • Skyfall • Someone Like You • When We Were Young.

00172162 1 Piano, 4 Hands..............$14.99

THE BEATLES FOR PIANO DUET
Intermediate Level
arr. Eric Baumgartner

Eight great Beatles' songs arranged for piano duet! Titles: Blackbird • Come Together • In My Life • Lucy in the Sky with Diamonds • Michelle • Ob-la-di, Ob-la-da • While My Guitar Gently Weeps • Yellow Submarine.

00275877 1 Piano, 4 Hands..............$14.99

THE BIG BOOK OF PIANO DUETS

24 great piano duet arrangements! Includes: Beauty and the Beast • Clocks • Edelweiss • Georgia on My Mind • He's a Pirate • Let It Go • Linus and Lucy • Moon River • Yellow Submarine • You are the Sunshine of My Life • and more!

00232851 1 Piano, 4 Hands..............$17.99

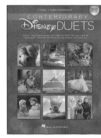

CONTEMPORARY DISNEY DUETS
Intermediate Level

8 great Disney duets: Evermore (from Beauty and the Beast) • How Does a Moment Last Forever (from Beauty and the Beast) • How Far I'll Go (from Moana) • Lava • Let It Go (from Frozen) • Proud Corazon (from Coco) • Remember Me (from Coco) • You're Welcome (from Moana).

00285562 1 Piano, 4 Hands..............$12.99

EASY CLASSICAL DUETS
Book/Online Audio
Willis Music

7 great piano duets to perform at a recital, play-for-fun, or sightread: By the Beautiful Blue Danube (Strauss) • Eine kleine Nachtmusik (Mozart) • Hungarian Rhapsody No. 5 (Liszt) • Morning from Peer Gynt (Grieg) • Rondeau (Mouret) • Sleeping Beauty Waltz (Tchaikovsky) • Surprise Symphony (Haydn). Includes online audio tracks for the primo and secondo part for download or streaming.

00145767 1 Piano, 4 Hands..............$12.99

FAVORITE DISNEY SONGS FOR PIANO DUET
Early Intermediate Level

8 great Disney songs creatively arranged for piano duet: Can You Feel the Love Tonight • Do You Want to Build a Snowman • A Dream Is a Wish Your Heart Makes • Supercalifragilisticexpialidocious • That's How You Know • When Will My Life Begin? • You'll Be in My Heart • You've Got a Friend in Me.

00285563 1 Piano, 4 Hands..............$14.99

FIRST 50 PIANO DUETS YOU SHOULD PLAY

Includes: Autumn Leaves • Bridge over Troubled Water • Chopsticks • Fields of Gold • Hallelujah • Imagine • Lean on Me • Theme from "New York, New York" • Over the Rainbow • Peaceful Easy Feeling • Singin' in the Rain • A Thousand Years • What the World Needs Now Is Love • You Raise Me Up • and more.

00276571 1 Piano, 4 Hands..............$24.99

GOSPEL DUETS
The Phillip Keveren Series

Eight inspiring hymns arranged by Phillip Keveren for one piano, four hands, including: Church in the Wildwood • His Eye Is on the Sparrow • Just a Closer Walk with Thee • The Old Rugged Cross • Shall We Gather at the River? • There Is Power in the Blood • When the Roll Is Called up Yonder.

00295099 1 Piano, 4 Hands..............$12.99

THE GREATEST SHOWMAN
by Benj Pasek & Justin Paul
Intermediate Level

Creative piano duet arrangements for the songs: Come Alive • From Now On • The Greatest Show • A Million Dreams • Never Enough • The Other Side • Rewrite the Stars • This Is Me • Tightrope.

00295078 1 Piano, 4 Hands..............$16.99

BILLY JOEL FOR PIANO DUET
Intermediate Level

8 of the Piano Man's greatest hits – perfect as recital encores, or just for fun! Titles: It's Still Rock and Roll to Me • Just the Way You Are • The Longest Time • My Life • New York State of Mind • Piano Man • She's Always a Woman • Uptown Girl.

00141139 1 Piano, 4 Hands..............$14.99

HEART AND SOUL & OTHER DUET FAVORITES

8 fun duets arranged for two people playing on one piano. Includes: Any Dream Will Do • Chopsticks • Heart and Soul • Music! Music! Music! (Put Another Nickel In) • On Top of Spaghetti • Raiders March • The Rainbow Connection • Y.M.C.A..

00290541 1 Piano, 4 Hands..............$12.99

RHAPSODY IN BLUE
George Gershwin/
arr. Brent Edstrom

Originally written for piano and jazz band, "Rhapsody in Blue" was later orchestrated by Ferde Grofe. This intimate adaptation for piano duet delivers access to advancing pianists and provides an exciting musical collaboration and adventure!

00125150 1 Piano, 4 Hands..............$14.99

RIVER FLOWS IN YOU & OTHER SONGS FOR PIANO DUET
Intermediate Level

10 great songs including the title song and: All of Me (Piano Guys) • Bella's Lullaby • Beyond • Chariots of Fire • Dawn • Forrest Gump - Main Title (Feather Theme) • Primavera • Somewhere in Time • Watermark.

00141055 1 Piano, 4 Hands..............$12.99

TOP HITS FOR EASY PIANO DUET
Book/Online Audio
arr. David Pearl

10 great songs with backing tracks: Despacito (Justin Bieber ft. Luis Fonsi & Daddy Yankee) • Havana (Camila Cabello ft. Young Thug • High Hopes (Panic! At the Disco) • A Million Dreams (*The Greatest Showman*) • Perfect (Ed Sheeran) • Senorita (Camila Cabello & Shawn Mendes) • Shallow (Lady Gaga & Bradley Cooper) • Someone You Loved (Lewis Capaldi) • Speechless (*Aladdin*) • Sucker (Jonas Brothers).

00326133 1 Piano, 4 Hands..............$12.99

HAL•LEONARD®
www.halleonard.com